SURVIVAL CHALLENGE

STRANDED!

Could YOU find shelter in the world's wildest places?

STEPHANIE TURNBULL

A+

Smart Apple Media

Published by Smart Apple Media,
an imprint of Black Rabbit Books
P.O. Box 3263, Mankato, Minnesota, 56002
www.blackrabbitbooks.com

Designed and illustrated by Guy Callaby
Edited by Mary-Jane Wilkins

Cataloging-in-Publication Data is available from the Library of Congress

ISBN 978-1-62588-217-2

Photo acknowledgements
t = top; c = center; b = bottom; r = right; l = left
folio image Olga Ryabtsova/Thinkstock; 2t Africa Studio,
b jurra8; 3 MountainHardcore; 4t Tom Middleton, b Galyna
Andrushko; 5t Dr. Morley Read, c Scott E Read, b David Varga;
6 Nejron Photo; 7c and b Dr. Morley Read/Shutterstock;
8 Maxim Toporskiy/Thinkstock; 10 Kropotov Andrey;
11 Ales Liska; 12 Phoric; 14t Stephane Bidouze, c Ryan M. Bolton, l alicedaniel;
15 SW_Stock; 16 Yuriy Kulik; 17 Ivan Pavlov; 18 Michel Cecconi, bc Iasha,
br trekandshoot; 10t My Good Images, c Paleka; 21 Tom Curtis;
23 Vitaly Maksimchuk
Cover t Jupiterimages/Thinkstock, b Benjamin Haas/Shutterstock

Printed in China

DAD0056
032014
9 8 7 6 5 4 3 2 1

CONTENTS

TAKE THE CHALLENGE

Imagine you're an intrepid traveler trekking through deep woods, dense rainforest, icy Arctic wastes or a vast, barren desert.

Things aren't going well. You're exhausted, lonely and miles from base camp. Pausing to rest your aching limbs, you realize with a shock how late it is. Shadows deepen, the temperature drops and eerie animal noises echo all around. The horrible truth sinks in—you're stranded in the wilderness.

Your challenge is to find shelter—fast. Can you do it?

It's easy to lose your way in the desert—and hard to find shelter.

Rainforests are hot, steamy and teeming
with wildlife. So where's a safe place to camp?

Could you survive a night in
rugged mountains, where the wind
howls and cougars (left) prowl?

LOOK AROUND YOU

First things first: don't panic. To make it through the night alive, you need to think clearly. Take a good look around and pick the best spot to make camp.

Make sure you're nowhere near a cliff edge like this when it's dark!

HIGH OR LOW?

If you're high on a cliff and exposed to the wind, head for lower, more sheltered ground. But don't go too low! Cold air sinks at night, so the lower you are, the chillier it will get. Look for a sheltered spot near a line of trees or raised ground.

Some valleys trap cold air on clear, still nights, so fog and frost form.

Cold air

Fog

Frost

Mountaineer Maurice Herzog was climbing Annapurna, in the Himalayas, when he got lost in mist and camped overnight in a narrow **crevasse**. In the morning, he heard a hissing sound—and suddenly a huge avalanche of snow buried him and his shelter! Amazingly, he managed to dig his way out.

FIND OPEN SPACES

Stuck in dense, dripping rainforest? Head for an open area to avoid getting damp during the night—and to prevent branches (or animals) falling on you as you sleep. Choose a patch of flat ground that's not too uncomfortable to lie on.

⟳ Move away from big trees to find drier, brighter areas.

Sleeping near an ant hill is not recommended.

WATCH FOR WATER

Set up camp near water for cooking and washing, but don't get too close. If a river or stream floods in bad weather, you could wake up wet—or find yourself being swept away with the water!

Heavy rain can turn gentle streams into raging rivers.

SET UP A TENT

You've selected your spot, so now put up your tent. If you've practiced this a few times you'll be able to do it quickly.

⋔ A well-pitched tent will withstand heavy snow and strong winds, especially if it is on flat ground in a sheltered spot.

Hiker Steve Thibeault was setting up his tent in a North Carolina forest when he realized he'd forgotten to pack tent poles. Instead, he strung rope between two trees, hung the tent over it and secured the ends. His quick thinking saved the day —and his shelter kept him safe all night.

REAL LIFE SURVIVAL

TENT TYPES

There are several kinds of tents. The most basic is an A-shaped ridge tent. This isn't very roomy, but it is strong.

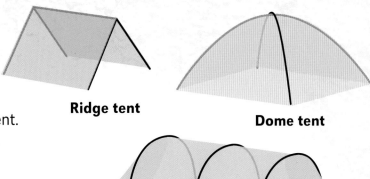

Ridge tent

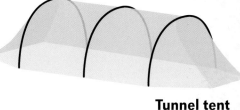

Dome tent

Tunnel tents have more space, but their shape makes them less stable in high winds.

Tunnel tent

Dome-shaped tents are strong and spacious, but they are heavy to carry, and can be tricky to put up.

THINK SMART

Pitch your tent with the entrance away from the wind. Dig a small drainage trench or ditch around it so water can run away. Make sure all the pegs are secure and there are no rips in the canvas.

☝ *In snow, add extra **insulation** by covering your tent with a frame of branches and a layer of snow.*

USE NATURAL SHELTER

What if you hadn't planned to be out long, and don't have a tent? Don't despair—perhaps you can find a natural shelter to use. It might not be comfortable, but you can't afford to be fussy!

LOOK FOR TREES

There are lots of natural shelters in forests. Crawl inside a hollow tree, or lie in the shelter of a fallen tree with a large spread of roots or branches. It's pretty basic, but it will protect you from wind and rain.

⟲ Hollows like this make great shelters. Sit on your backpack to avoid getting damp.

CRAWL IN A CAVE

Caves make ideal emergency shelters. Some are huge underground mazes, so stay near the entrance to avoid getting lost or wedged in a tunnel. Remember that animals take shelter in caves, so check it's empty before you settle down for the night. Bears don't like to share!

COVER UP

Can't see a hollow tree or cave? How about taking shelter under big bushes or piles of logs or leaves? If the ground is dry, curl up in a hollow on a pile of leaves. You can collect branches to rest over the top.

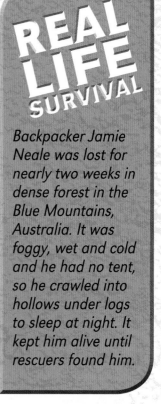

BUILD A FOREST HUT

Forests are full of materials for building a shelter. The more effort you put in, the more comfortable you'll be, but keep an eye on the sky and finish well before night falls or bad weather comes.

↻ *Pine branches piled on a frame are good for keeping out rain and wind.*

MAKE A LEAN-TO
A lean-to is a simple shelter made from branches propped against something solid.

1. Lean ten or more long, straight branches against a bank or large tree. Make sure the space is big enough to lie in.

2. Weave bendy twigs, fir branches, reeds or long grasses between the sticks, then fill the gaps with dead leaves. If it's snowy, pile snow on top.

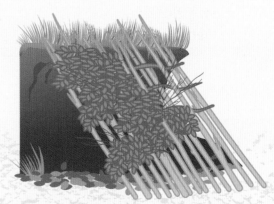

Richard Proenneke was a farm worker who built a log cabin in the Alaskan forest and lived there for 30 years. He made his own furniture using hand tools, many of which he also crafted himself. He became famous for his **bushcraft** skills and people still visit his log cabin today.

MAKE A DEBRIS HUT

A debris hut uses the same materials as a lean-to, but it stands alone.

1. Dig a shallow trench big enough to lie in.

2. Line it with sticks and dry leaves.

3. Make a frame with two strong, forked branches and one long, thick branch.

4. Rest shorter branches on either side of the frame, then cover with leaves and other vegetation.

MAKE A JUNGLE SHELTER

he rainforest is a pretty soggy place. Your shelter needs a thick base of branches to keep you off the damp ground, and a sturdy roof to protect you from torrential downpours.

➡ *Steer clear of shady places as snakes shelter there in piles of logs or leaves.*

USE YOUR KNIFE
The good news is that there are two fantastic building materials in the jungle—long, straight **bamboo** stems and huge, thick palm leaves. The bad news is that you need a knife to cut them. Did you bring one?

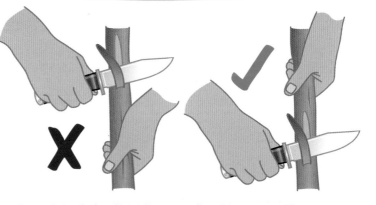

Concentrate when using a knife. Always cut away from your body, and keep your fingers out of the way.

14

FINE FRAMES

Bamboo poles make a strong, neat lean-to (see page 12) or frame. Lash the stems together with long, thick vines.

To add a roof, split palm leaves in half down the middle...

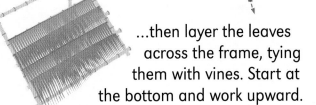

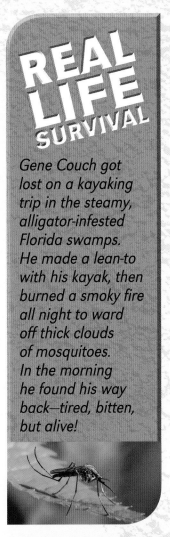

...then layer the leaves across the frame, tying them with vines. Start at the bottom and work upward.

HANDY HAMMOCKS

Packed a hammock? Good job! These make ideal jungle beds as you can tie them between two trees and stay off wet ground. String a **tarpaulin** over the top as a roof and add a **mosquito net** so you don't get nibbled in the night. Perfect!

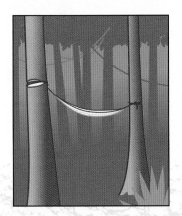

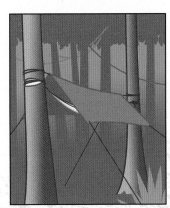

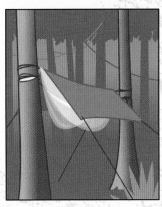

You won't last long in the desert without shelter. It's blisteringly hot by day and perishingly cold by night. Strong winds whip up blinding sandstorms and sudden rain causes **flash floods**. But how do you make a shelter when all you can see is sand?

KEEP COOL!

Look for trees, rocky cliffs or hollows between sand dunes that may create shadows. Head for shade and try to rest as much as possible. Take regular sips of water and stay calm.

USE A TARP

A tarpaulin or blanket in your backpack could save your life. Use it to make a lean-to, and secure it with rocks.

If you find two trees, string rope between them, hang the tarpaulin over the top and weigh down the ends. If you don't have rope, tear a T-shirt into strips to make a cord.

No trees or rocks? Dig a trench in the sand to lie in. Pull the tarpaulin over you, leaving a gap to breathe. You'll be hot and miserable, but it beats sitting in the sun.

Berber people in North Africa shelter from desert sandstorms in an unusual place—inside dead camels! They slice off the skin, remove the guts and crawl inside the huge carcass with the skin as a blanket. It's a very effective (if smelly) refuge.

REAL LIFE SURVIVAL

*For tips on finding water in the desert, you need a copy of **Survival Challenge: Thirsty!***

DIG INTO SNOW

Think an igloo is the best emergency snow shelter? Think again. Unless you have hours to spare, a special saw to cut blocks of snow, and a friend to help you lay and shape each one, then forget it. Don't build—dig.

Igloos are fantastic shelters, but building them is best left to the experts!

DIGGING BASICS

Find something to dig with. Use a shovel, ice axe, snowshoe or even a plastic container from your backpack. Brush snow off your clothes as you work to avoid it soaking through and leaving you wet and shivering.

SNOW CAVES

In mountains, look for deep drifts of snow blown against rock faces. Hollow out a space just big enough for you and your gear.

Poke air holes through the top of your cave, then block the entrance with your backpack or a block of snow. Cold air sinks, so make a raised bed to sleep on, and lie on spare clothes to stay warm and dry.

COVERED TRENCHES

In flat, exposed places such as the Arctic, dig a trench and line it with spare clothes or pine needles.

Lay branches over the trench and cover them with vegetation or snow. Leave a gap for ventilation (and to crawl inside).

Air hole

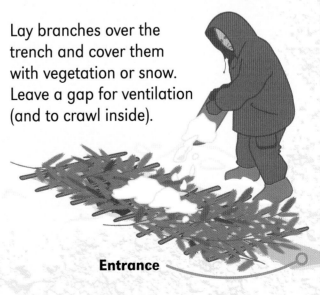

Entrance

GET COMFORTABLE

You're safe and dry inside your emergency shelter. Good job! Here are a few tips to get you through the long night ahead.

LIGHT A FIRE

If you have space outside, make a small fire for warmth and light. But don't build it so close that it sets your shelter alight— and *never* make a fire inside. It will use up **oxygen** and give off smoke and harmful gases.

⟳ Hot stones in a tin help warm your shelter. Don't burn yourself!

*Not sure how to make a fire? Read another book in this series, **Survival Challenge: Cold!***

KEEP CLEAN

Feel like freshening up? Boil water in a pot over your fire then add it to a bowl of crushed pine needles. When it's cool, strain it through a clean sock and gargle with it. The **antiseptic** properties of pine needles will leave your mouth clean and fresh.

In the desert, look for yucca plants like these and cut a piece of root.

Add water and pound the root with a stone.

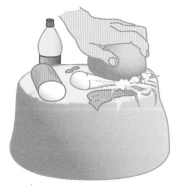

Hey presto—soap!

STAY SNUG

Make your shelter cozier by plugging gaps in the sides with mud, leaves, turf or moss. Don't forget to leave a few ventilation holes! And by the way, moss also makes good toilet paper. Could come in handy...

A scientist and explorer named Fridtjof Nansen once spent a whole winter in a stone hut on an icy island in the Arctic Ocean. To keep his skin clean, he scoured it with moss and sand. He also scraped off grease with a knife and used the fat as fuel. Nice!

REAL LIFE SURVIVAL

21

antiseptic
A substance that destroys harmful bacteria or stops them growing.

bamboo
A type of strong, hollow plant stem that is often used as a building material.

Berber
A member of a group of people from North Africa. Many Berbers live in tribes who travel from place to place with herds of animals.

bushcraft
Skills and knowledge that you need to survive in the wilderness.

crevasse
A deep crack in a mass of ice.

flash flood
A sudden flood caused by short-lived but very heavy rain.

insulation
Materials that are used to prevent heat escaping as it rises.

mosquito net
A fine mesh sheet that lets air in, but keeps mosquitoes and other insects out. Mosquitoes can carry diseases such as malaria.

oxygen
An invisible gas in the air around us. We need oxygen to breathe and fires need it to burn.

tarpaulin
A heavy, waterproof sheet, often made of canvas, with small holes around the edges for attaching rope.

www.wildwoodsurvival.com/survival/shelter/index.html
All kinds of wilderness shelters–some basic, others more complicated.

www.wilderness-survival-skills.com/survivalshelter.html
Top tips for finding or making quick, safe shelters.

www.thesurvivalexpert.co.uk/SurvivalShelterCategory.html
How to make emergency shelters, plus plenty more survival tips.

INDEX